TENDER WRITING

A Simple, Clear and Concise Guide

CAROLINE SAVAGE

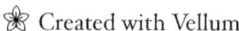 Created with Vellum

For my Dad

CONTENTS

OVERVIEW

Thank you for purchasing Tender Writing: A Simple, Clear and Concise Guide, the second book in the Simple, Clear and Concise series. Tender Writing provides an overview of my tender writing process and is aimed at tender writers working in the not for profit, the small business and the social enterprise who seek to sell their products or services to government or larger organisations in response to a tender.

Tenders are part of a service or product ***procurement*** process – a purchase. The purchase process may be broken down into stages or adapted to address particular aspects of the organisational need. It may include a stage where government or the larger organisation seeks to gauge the interest of suppliers. This is a funnelling stage – the expression of interest - to select the best pool of applicants before going to a full tender process. It may be a request for a specific activity and includes the request for tender **(RFT)**, applications, information, offers, proposals, quotations and services. Tender Writing details the process for the development of an ***application/bid*** for a full tender response to the RFT and can be refined to meet the other specific activities under its generalised heading.

For a business, the lure of the government tender is appealing. Where else can businesses apply for secured income for their business activities for a fixed project, for a fixed time and for a fixed price? There is a note of caution here and it is only if your application/bid is well planned, professional and meets the needs of the procuring government or large organisation - referred to as the ***organisation*** from this point forward.

For the not-for-profit, governments are moving from granting money based on planned outcomes to a formal procurement of services/products and results-based funding within a contractual environment. Some tender applications will still feel like you are applying for a grant however, the expectations, professional approach and the nature of the contracts have changed. There may be specific contract terms for non-performance where a fixed amount of money is held back until the contract is delivered, typically a percentage of the full award, a specific claw back provision where money already paid must be repaid, a termination clause where the contract will cease or a service level agreement where non-performance is met with fiscal penalties.

Not-for-profits will continue to experience this change in the grants' environment and the tender process already underway will continue to harmonise with the procurement process demanded of business. For this reason, from this point forward in the book whether you are a small business, not-for-profit or a social venture, the text will refer to the ***business***.

Tenders are not a get-rich-quick scheme. They require you to understand the political environment, link in to local needs and to provide evidence of your corporate responsibility to not only the service/product you are providing but also the work-force and community you employ and live within. The tender response can also form a binding contract, if you are successful.

Unlike the medium to large business sector, the process of tender writing tends to fall to people with other roles, where writing tenders is not necessarily within their skill set. Whereas, my expertise derives from my employment in the government, universities and the not for profit sector as a project developer and manager including roles as a tender and grant writer and as an assessor with Government departments.

I have been writing to secure funding for over 20 years in an international environment. I have secured millions of dollars in funding, and this has allowed me to develop projects from conception to completion and some with project activity extending on with additional and renewed funding streams. My aim is to share my tender writing process with you.

Tender Writing is set up in a similar way to the process of writing a response to a tender and, in doing so, will allow you to follow the flow of the RFT process. Tender Writing will guide you through the RFT by:

- examining the tender environment
- identifying your needs as a writer
- preparing you for the tendering process
- helping you to identify tenders
- working through the tender assessment process
- identifying the research requirements
- planning your project
- preparing your budget
- identifying your writing style

- responding to the questions
- identifying referees
- identifying other documentation that may be required
- detailing the editing and proofing processes
- understanding the impact of the sign-off and submission
- the post assessment process

This book does not replace the RFT. Rather, it supports you in responding to the tender and provides you with some thoughts and inspiration from a mentor to guide you through the process.

Of course, there is no guarantee of a tender award. It shares a process of writing a tender that worked for me. It takes input from you to make this happen by improving your own, and your team's skills to improve your success rate.

Enough with the introduction, it is time to start writing. Enjoy the book and I would appreciate it if you would rate it at the end. Your rating gives people a real-world view of the usefulness of the information and will help them to make a choice as to whether the book is for them.

If there are any questions remaining after reading this book, feel free to contact me at www.grantandtenderwriting.com via the contact page or link in with the community forum on the same website.

CHECKLIST

- Do you understand the format of the book?
- Do you know where to go for additional information from the author?
- Have you noted the key terms for the rest of the book?

THE RFT ENVIRONMENT

Tenders are the way government or other organisations carry out procurement activities. In other words, it is their formal process of obtaining or acquiring services or products.

Tenders offer a clear process of governance, as in there are internal rules and controls, to underpin the procurement process. That includes opening a tender in certain publications, evaluating a tender in a fair and unbiased way and the final selection and award of the tender to the successful organisation. It can extend into the management of the ongoing procurement with a service level agreement. The tender governance process ensures probity, fairness and transparency for the businesses bidding for the tender.

In an active tender process, a planned procurement is published or gazetted with a clear indication of when the tender is likely to open. This is followed by the tender notification or the RFT, which has the tender name, reference number, whether it is an open, closed or multi-staged tender, the tender opening date, closing date and aim of the tender. Attached to the RFT will be the tender documents and a way to contact the organisation. The ability to contact the organisation has a time-limited contact period. This is to allow questions to be submitted and answered and circulated to the businesses tendering in good time to make necessary changes to their application/bid. Conditions are always clearly stated in the RFT and this includes the deadline, which is normally a matter of weeks, from the tender opening to closing. Whilst the tender remains open, addendum will be posted with additional information. Any questions posed to the organisation will be circulated within the addendum. It is the applicant business's responsibility to be aware of new addendum activity.

In the normal process of the tender, business is required to sign into the portal to obtain the RFT documentation. The email you register with is the one the organisation will use to advise of ongoing activity in the current tender's process.

The tender environment is highly competitive especially when the tender is classed as an open 'open to all' tender or a multi-staged tender. Multi-staged tenders are highly competitive at all stages. The organisation will seek applications/bids from a wide pool of businesses and funnel the pool of businesses through levels of tender stages. In some cases, the tender is classed as a closed tender and that is because it relates to a very small pool of potential business applicants. For example, it may be that it is in relation to the provision of a specialist service and the organisation plans to target business with a particular focus or it is a renewal of a tender and the organisation is targeting those businesses they have funded in the previous round.

The tender environment is a commercial contract. The organisation will demand value for money. Now this does not mean to say that they are looking for the cheapest option. They are looking for the most viable option and the onus is on your business to communicate the reasons why you can provide what the organisation needs. It may be based on your pricing, risk mitigation, innovation or the level of product/service you offer. The organisation will examine your viability as a business, your track record and how you have delivered in the past, as a guide to how you would deliver in the future.

That is not to say a new business cannot break into the tender environment but it does mean that you will have to show your viability, potential and value differentiator to stand out from your more established competitors. One area where this is key is in relation to corporate responsibility and interaction and impact with your local community. This includes, but it is not limited to, how you engage your local community workforce and your commitment to environmental sustainability. Some organisations include social clauses into their procurement process. If this is the case in a tender you are applying/bidding for, the assessment is skewed towards businesses who adapt to local demand, are innovators and change makers in response to their community's current and future local needs. For example, where unemployment is at an all-time high, the government department will request the product/service provision response to include local employment initiatives. Social clauses are set to become more and more common, as there is an ongoing drive to have social clauses incorporated into many government tenders.

The organisation will seek excellence and an ongoing quality management process. There may be specific questions in the tender document addressing this or may be implied from in the nature of your business process.

The tender environment requires your business to be viable and a tender might be the way your business plans to maintain viability. Some organisations are finding it really tough financially and they require some sort of ongoing funding in the form of a tender or a grant. Grants to business are not common. Business is expected to strive for viability and growth. The tender offers you a chance to demonstrate your viability, secure the award, and have a firm base of work from which to grow your business. Similarly, a planned social venture may be better to develop the start-up around a tender award. Social ventures may be able to access seed funding if they have a viable business. The tender can be the main source of activity to give the social venture a ready-made customer. By doing this, the social venture will start with stability from the get-go and will be able to use that as a launch-pad to deliver their services and values on a long-term basis. However, it is not a solution to a failing business. If your business is not viable or you have not developed the requisite business plans and projections, you will be setting yourself up for failure if you win the tender with regards to the penalties and the consequences set out in a contract.

Under a tender you will be contractually bound, if successful, to deliver what you said you are going to do by a specific time and for a specific cost. The organisation normally provides a draft contract as part of the RFT. They may allow you to negotiate terms or it may be a binding contract where no changes will be allowed. As a business, you need to understand you are contractually bound to the terms of the award and understand what you are contractually bound to deliver or perform.

Tenders tend to be large, technical projects. They usually require a team approach to the procurement and acquisition in relation to your services or products and that extends to the tender application process. The cost implications of the development of an application/bid will rest with the business and, as the activity predates the tender award, will not be recoverable as an eligible cost. This places a considerable investment expectation on your business to develop an end to end tender application/bid with an uncertain chance of winning the tender. This is a business risk and it is not the only one.

Another risk is to understand the tender environment is also open to scams. Some scammers will promise you the world and yet will deliver nothing. This is a *buyer beware* moment and a reminder to check with your local business development department to understand what the current scams are around tenders and grants. I have included grants in that request for information because quite often these scamming organisations will ask for a fee from you in exchange for a worthless promise to securing additional 'funding'.

The tender environment provides information for free via the organisation's website or via an agency they subscribe to. Register on each site or portal to keep up to date with the tenders as they are listed. In addition, organisations sometimes offer free information sessions to help you understand their planned procurements and to help strengthen your skills in making an application/bid under their tender procurement process. If you have these opportunities, use them. The information and the networking at these events is pivotal to your future success in the tender environment.

With so many new skill requirements, you may consider using an external consultant to write the tender for you. This is entirely a business decision. Your will need to consider the following when engaging an external consultant. The first issue is whether they are working just for you or whether they will be submitting other tenders for other businesses in the same tender round. Clearly you want them just working for you and not working with your competition. Ask what their success rate is in the tender environment and if they have written in your area of procurement before. They may be able to provide examples, obviously subject to confidentiality by blanking out key information. Tender consultants are not cheap to engage but their expertise in the tender can outweigh their costs. The earlier you make the decision to engage them, the better the result for your business as most times, they will help set up the processes for the tender, as well as do the actual writing. That said, this book is about *you* learning to write tenders.

It is also about you gauging your, and your business's, suitability, capacity to tender, whether the tender process is a viable option for you, and what skills you, and your team, need to develop yourself to meet the rigour and requirements of the tender process.

CHECKLIST

- Do you understand what a tender is?
- Do you understand the tender process?
- Do you understand the implications and expectations of the tender process?
- Have you linked into organisations' tender sites and events to gain information and skills?
- Have you checked out potential scams in your area?

THE WRITER'S NEEDS

It is time to concentrate on your needs but before you do that, you need to take a good hard look at yourself as a tender writer. It is important to understand how much help you might need in the tender writing process, where you might get that help and who specifically may be able to help you.

Firstly though, I would like you to review your ethical viewpoint and stance on the tender writing process. This review, if you are employed as a writer, also includes the potential business you work with, or for. There is a professional expectation that you will only write one tender for one business at a time because in doing so, you will promote the profession in a positive light. Similarly, you have to ensure you share the business vision for the tender you are about to write to. Do you believe in the product, the people and the procurement? Writing tenders is not something to be done with little care or passion, but with a huge heart and excitement about the future ahead. Your words have the ability to keep your business viable, the staff supported and employed, whilst providing value for money and a long-term contract from the organisation you are tendering to. Passion alone though is not enough.

There is an expectation that you will have strong writing skills and will have a persuasive point of view to sway the organisation to your win theme detailing the overarching features and benefits that dictate the point of view of the tender. It may be that the review process takes in some constructive feedback or mentoring from another peer to provide you with honest feedback for strengths and areas for growth. It is not just the writing either.

As a tender writer, you will need:

- Active listening skills to gain an understanding of the distinct differences of the project from those involved, gauge their issues and hopes for the project.
- The ability to analyse multiple data sets,

reality testing and their factual representation in the application/bid.

- To be an innovative problem-solver and have a good understanding of conflict and dispute resolution for not just the tender, but the teams you are working with.

- To have strong communication and presentation skills for the tender process through to possible interactions with the organisation.

- Formal project management training to manage the tender process, the project development, planning and delivery. You will be constantly asked to monitor and track the progress of the tender/internal plans.

- Financial management skills with the ability to read budgets, understand fiscal modelling and to be able to translate that into the tender and to highlight potential issues that may arise.

- Computer literacy skills with, at a minimum, an understanding of the Microsoft365 suite of software, plus Adobe, other design and desktop publishing, project management software and other internal software including budgeting tools and many more.

Your ability to assess your skill-set at this stage of the tender process is pivotal to the success of the tender. You are not expected to know everything. You are expected to know where your strengths are, where you need additional training and where there is an opportunity to bring other team members in, to support you. It is not a sign of weakness to ask for help and to build a strong team around you. It is a sign of leadership that will continue to be required of you throughout the tender process.

That said, you need, at this stage, to consider your project team, your role within it and the impact of team dynamics and the internal project management process on you.

Tenders are by their very nature large projects. They may have a technical bias and will require, in most cases, a team approach for the procurement and acquisition of service/product that will be in operation long after the tender is submitted. Even if the tender is a small one, you have a responsibility to yourself to not be left alone in this process.

Development   the   application/bid   requires

constant management of the process and the people. Whether you lead the team, or are an active participant within it, your understanding of the team's role in the whole process and the expectations placed upon them will, if managed correctly, lead to a strong application/bid. The teams may be made up of people more senior than you and with other responsibilities taking up their time. It could be that the expectation is the majority of the work will fall to the writer and thus other team member's input can be minimal and submitted with little understanding of the time required to craft responses. Without strong leadership and management from you, it will result in late and low-quality information for the tender, unnecessary stress on the writer and the writing resulting in a low-quality application/bid. If this happens and it is all left to you, keep the communication flowing between yourself and the wider project team as opposed to trying to cope and ask for support.

Tender writing is a team effort and its strength and value will be in direct correlation to a responsive and proactive team.

With all the discussion around you, it is the perfect time to discuss your compensation for the work you carry out. It is easy if you are employed and the role is written into your job description. If not, it is time to get on one of the vacancy advertising sites such as Seek, CareerOne, or similar sites. Gauge the payments for vacancies in your field of expertise and the level of involvement you will be expected to manage. If you are self-employed, try and see what similar consultants are charging and see whether that covers you and your on-costs. Like any good tender, your rate needs to reflect the level of your involvement and a realistic assessment of the hours you will be working plus on-costs. I know some of my colleagues who have set a weekly rate based on 38 hours work only to realise too late that the employer classes their work week as a 60-80 hour week. This is not only ridiculous but it is contrary to your health and wellbeing.

Keeping with the health and wellbeing theme, you have a duty to your own health and safety during the tender process. Ensure that you have your work station and chair set up in the correct ergonomic way. Take regular breaks from the computer. Like my example with the 60-80 hour week above, examine your work-life balance and structure your workload to balance the needs of the tender and your personal needs. There will be times when you work extended hours. They should never become the norm. Burning out over writing tenders is not worth it.

Finally, ensure you have insurance in place to limit your liability and cover any risks associated with you or your business. We live in a litigious world and there are many risks you can mitigate with adequate insurance. The two you will require as a minimum are relating to the advice/services you offer as a tender writer and your interaction with other people.

Depending on your location, insurance to protect you as a provider of professional advice or a service is covered by either professional indemnity insurance, professional liability and errors and omissions insurance. It gives you some protection against civil law suits. Public liability covers you for events that may have an impact on third parties. Seek out professional advice in relation to having adequate insurance and cover for your business activities.

CHECKLIST

- Are you content that you share the ethical viewpoint and vision with your business?
- Have you realistically assessed your skills and training needs?
- Have you got a realistic expectation for compensation for the work you do?
- Have you assessed your work environment for your health and safety?
- Have you got the correct insurances in place?

PREPARING TO TENDER

There is quite a bit of work you can do in preparation for the tendering process as a tender writer. The work done in preparation will save you time as you enter the application/bid process and as you continue in your tendering journey. The information below relates to the business process preparation and the preparations in terms of the people employed or contracted to support you in that process. It is not an exhaustive list.

The Process - Generic paragraphs (boilerplate information)

Much information in your business is boilerplate

information. Boilerplate information is information that can be used again and again without much change. For example, how you achieved certain goals within the year, when the business was incorporated, corporate information in general such as annual reports. Boilerplate information is also called generic information in the tender environment. It includes generic paragraphs used again and again in the tender documents. These generic paragraphs can include:

- An acronym list for all of your organisation. This is a document that can sometimes be an appendix to the tender document and makes it easier for you to speak in the normal acronyms of your organisation. However, when putting these in the tender text, always put them in full in the first instance followed by the acronym in brackets and from there onwards use only the acronym in its normal format. See RFT in Chapter One as an example.
- Awards and recognition such as employer of choice and community champion activities.

- Compliance and compliance matrices demonstrating your adherence to Federal, State and local laws, rules and directions. You will need to ensure that you have the specific compliance for the tender, which may exceed the statutory ones.
- Illustrations, diagrams and corporate documentation relevant to your brand. Be aware some tendering forms do not allow for diagrams to be inserted, although you may be able to add them to appendices.
- Industry required certification such as ISO standards that you have achieved.
- Other accreditation, quality assurance and product information.
- Other information specific to your business including confidentiality agreements and other corporate documentation or templated information.
- Policies and procedures. Like the compliance point above, you may need to develop new policies and procedures to meet the requirements of the tender. For the smaller business, this may require a more rigid and structured framework. It can seem daunting; however, this

information is in the public domain and, with some investment of your time/money, it can be set up in a few months.

- Research and statistics, you have specific to your field of expertise. This can include internal research and external research.
- Staff roles, responsibilities and qualifications. Ask your human resources department to map the skills of your staff and have their job descriptions and resumes ready on file. This allows you to reference the project/tender/procurement teams and detail their skills and expertise to support the tender.
- Standard operating procedures and other workflow documents. These may be useful in project planning, timelines and budgets too.
- Style guide to support your business brand. You will want to ensure that everyone follows the business branding and extends that to the tender document. The RFT may demand you use the organisation's style guide but in any case, you or your writers and editors will want a definitive style guide to work with and towards.

As a business, you will have a wealth of information pertaining to your products/services. However, these documents tend to be written for a different audience and may need adapting to a sales focus/win theme. This way your generic paragraphs will define your value point difference to the organisation. Once adapted, the information can be saved into generic folder files on your computer network. This ensures anyone in the tender team can access the information. It may be worth protecting the information with master copies or password protection. This will give you some control in keeping the information current and, more importantly, accurate. With any generic document, it is worth setting in place regular review points. This gives you and your business peace of mind knowing the information is up-to-date and factual.

The Process - Concept Development

Other process elements you can have in place prior to tendering is a clear idea of what you will deliver as a product/service. The concept development is a great start to understand what you want to deliver, when you want to deliver it and with a rough idea of how much it is going to cost you to do that.

This is not the stage to do a full project plan. It is the time to consider what tender product or service you plan to tender for. Have a rough idea of the project and how it may work. Consider the key points of your corporate differentiation of your product/service. These are the factors that allow your business to stand out from your competition in regard to the concept you have in development. These also form the key arguments or win themes for an organisation to select you for the tender award. Have some idea of timelines and the potential impact of the tendering process and the tender on your current business operation, if awarded.

We will talk more about budgets later in the book, but for now have an idea of your basic overhead costs. Basic overhead costs are the costs that remain constant and are apportioned to each new activity, and the implications of future tenders on your assets and staffing needs.

A basic overview of the concept will help you to understand what tenders may suit your business and which ones will negatively impact on the business's financial and operational vision.

The Process - Internal Tender Process

The internal tender process is governed by your opportunity assessment (OA) pipeline. The pipeline is the process required by your business to consider planned and current tenders, discuss their viability, and sanction a decision as to whether to proceed – go, or not to proceed – no-go otherwise known as the go/no-go decision process and to allocate staff to carry out the works.

Like any major program of works, this needs to be project-managed. It can be managed from a simple Excel spreadsheet to a monumental policy and procedure document with formal internal management and project management software. As this book targets the small business, let's keep it simple.

Start by setting up an Excel document to collate the tenders you are considering. Enter the relevant information including the tender name, reference, website link, contact info, tender description, internal tender officer, date tender opened, date and time tender closes, OA stages as a drop-down box, (you can define these per your business requirements and they will include the process of the tender – identified, sent for decision, no-go, in progress, submitted, awarded, not awarded), OA Decision as in the go/no-go, text for general updates and information, amount applied for, date submitted, expected date of award notification, whether successful or not and a last box to determine the cost to your business to tender. With this information, you can manage the OA pipeline and you can also assess the cost implications of tendering based on your win rate (the proportion of costs to tender as a percentage of the amounts awarded) or the amounts you have secured through tendering.

It is also good practice to have a go/no–go matrix decision tool within a standardised document. The decision tool places information relevant to your business to be able to make a consistent decision as to the viability of the tender. This may include the planned project, the impact on the business in terms of staff and assets, legal, financial, risk information, planned project, costings to prepare, potential profit, etc. You may find there are key decision points important to you and you can add in tools to make it easier for staff to add their information such as a value proposition tool (the sales message), a risk assessment matrix, etc. Alongside the tools you will need to define the staff involved in the OA pipeline and those with authority to give the go/no-go on the decision to tender or not.

Behind the OA Pipeline you will need to have a tender strategy for both the long term and short term needs of your business. Document your business's vision for the tenders, the organisations you want to target, how many you want to apply for, when you want to apply for them and the growth/profit you expect to generate. This will make the go/no-go decision much easier to assess.

The People

Preparing people for the tendering process can be addressed when you are preparing to tender.

In the previous chapter, we looked at the skills of the writer and asked you to consider any skill deficits you may have. If there are skill deficits in the team, training can be put in place to ensure the writer/project team is ready to tender and a mentor may be engaged to support writing staff new to the process so as to enable them to gain the confidence and skills for the tendering process.

Seek support from external experts including the organisations you are tendering to. Do not be afraid to network with your government departments and see if there is an employee there who can legitimately support you to strengthen yourselves in preparation to tender. Clearly, they will not breach any probity in relation to tenders but they are always keen to ensure they have a strong applicant pool and will work with all applicants in the same way to strengthen their skills.

Identify your project team early. This way, like the writer, you can check out whether you have got any gaps in the team's membership or skill-set. It is also a time for some team building meetings to ensure the team is well coordinated and anticipating the urgency and expectations around their part in the process. This is especially important in relation to timelines and expectations for the team to deliver quality responses.

Consider the professional team members and how you will incorporate their knowledge and expertise into the project team and the OA pipeline. This includes your:

- Legal teams who will provide advice on confidentiality agreements, contracts implications, service level agreements and potential for retention of awarded funds for non-compliance, caveats for any unplanned changes, procurement and supply chain issues as well as conflict and dispute resolution.
- Accountants or legal or financial team. There have been many incidents of people

gaining the tender and going bankrupt in the process, only for the tender to be passed on to another business. This would be an awful experience if that were your business, which is where the financial team comes in, as they will model the planned procurements for the tender to ensure you are protected, as far as possible, from this.

- Other experts including occupational health and safety, human resources, procurement officers and those experts within your business who are fundamental to the process of your business.

The inclusion of the professional team members from an early stage is pivotal to the opportunity assessment. Without their expertise, a tender cannot be realistically considered for its viability. It is quite possible that you may have to walk away from some tenders because they are just not viable to deliver for the allocated budget or within your capacity.

Identify the project plan review team at this time. They will have some synergy with a project team and it will be their job to ensure any project plans developed in readiness for the tender are consistent with the organisational needs as described in the RFT, are meeting the project aims and objectives and will be there to ensure the subsequent application/bid is accurate, achievable and can be delivered on time and on budget.

It is also the time to identify people for the editing/proofing team. These editors/reviewers will need to be free from the writing process, as they need to have a fresh set of eyes to edit/review the documentation. Again, identifying them early ensures they are kept clear of the project teams and can set aside time in readiness for their role within the project.

Identify your potential partners and any supply chain and procurement needs. By doing this, you will have access to early stage costings. This includes the cost of printers, editors, couriers and designers. Applications/bids will require a professional standard of design and branding as well as the potential for delivery by courier.

There is much you can do in preparation for the tendering process. Preparation gives you a head start for when the tender opens and, if you have a short turnaround to the closing date, a head start on the competition. No time is lost in preparation and the stronger your work in this area, the stronger your tender will be.

As I said at the start of this chapter, this is not

meant to be an exhaustive list. The preparation process will always be a work in progress with ongoing reviews and updates, as well as continued alignment of the information to your business's tendering environment. This chapter is a start to ensure you have quick access to relevant information.

CHECKLIST

- Have you identified your generic information (boilerplate information)?
- Have you updated it to meet the tendering process?
- Have you got a rough idea of your product/service concept?
- Have you developed an OA pipeline process?
- Have you developed your tender strategy document?
- Have you defined, up-skilled, and informed your staff of the tendering timeline?
- Have you allocated staff roles and teams?

TENDER IDENTIFICATION

Tender information is published with FREE access on the organisation's website or on an aggregate portal they elect to use. There are companies out there who will aggregate this information for you and their reach is normally quite extensive. These aggregate companies will normally have a subscription service allowing you to highlight the areas you are interested in tendering for and they provide a database environment to search for planned and current tenders. The decision to use a company to aggregate the information is one normally based on cost. The time they save you in searching can be quite cost-efficient and that is a business decision for you whether you subscribe to them.

If you are a smaller business and you are looking

for local tenders and contracts to apply for, then it might be easier to register with your State, Federal and Local Government departments relevant to your local area and procurement plans. Each of those departments of government have a free portal where you can register and highlight the information you would like to receive notices on. They will have a daily email digest of new tenders. Make time to review the new tenders published on a daily basis, as each day missed from the notice of an open tender is a day that eats into your response time.

When you enter into the tender website, you will see current tenders comprising of open, multi-staged and closed tenders. Open tenders which are 'open for all suppliers', multi-staged tenders are used to reduce the pool of businesses in a funnel by means of expressions of interest and the invitation to proceed to the next stage based on merit, and closed tenders where only selected suppliers are invited to tender. This is quite confusing because you may think a closed tender would be one that has expired. Expired tenders are classed as 'tenders under review' and then 'accepted tenders' or a similar name depending on the organisation. There are also planned procurements on the site. They are formally notified so that businesses have time to prepare for the upcoming tendering process.

When you click on a tender of interest you will see the one page summary of the tender. It will state the name and reference number, the opening day and the time and date the tender closes. You will see that quite often there is a short period of time to work on them. I have seen some tenders where there was only one week to get the tender together and there are others which tend to be around the three-week mark or longer. The close date and time is a hard deadline. If you are halfway through submitting your tender and the deadline passes, you will just be closed out of the portal and the partial application will drop off the system.

Take some time to research your preferred supply area and understand how the organisation you will be tendering to, manage their process. Know whether the organisation offers planned procurement information or determine if their opening of the tender to the close time is a certain length of time on every occasion or differs. Examine the current tender documents and see what level of work is required. This will give you a realistic view of their procurement, how much information they provide you on how the tender will be assessed, what to expect in the writing and even down to the specifics such as, how much compliance you will be expected to meet to be eligible to tender.

Also check out the awarded tenders. These are usually gazetted and publicly available and you will be able to see the businesses that have been successful. You can check out their websites, their annual reports and policies as well as processes, provided they are publicly available, so as to gauge what it took for them to be successful. Check out their standing in the community and try to understand what made them stand out in the tender process.

Tender identification is more than just finding a tender to apply for. It is about understanding the process of the particular organisation you will be tendering to and understanding your potential competition and their track record and standing with the organisation. With this information, you will be able to make a qualified decision that will help place your business in the best position to win the tender.

CHECKLIST

- Do you know where to find planned and open tenders?
- Have you registered in your area of interest on all sites?
- Do you have a rough idea of your local tender process and timelines?
- Have you researched previous tenders and the businesses they have been awarded to?
- Do you know where you are best placed to win the tender?

TENDER IDENTIFIED - WHAT'S NEXT?

With your tender identified, it is now time to start the tender writing process. This chapter relates to the administration of the tender and setting the tender administration folders up in the correct format.

The administration phase is based on a process I used while I was employed to project manage large infrastructure projects. I have adapted it to work on small-scale projects and equally it can be scaled up, if required. I am sure you can tweak it in the future to get it right for you. And trust me, the system works. The uniformity of the process means anyone in your organisation can pick it up and know where to locate everything and exactly where you are at in the opportunity pipeline process. This is pivotal. Writers are not immune to illness or sudden and unexpected events taking them away from work. The more rigid your administration, the easier it is to maintain continuity of works.

The first stage in the administration process is to set up the files on your computer to keep the tender in a consolidated workflow. The first folder is the name of the tender. You may add to your opportunity pipeline, information to the name or follow the file naming conventions of your business. Under that folder I create the following sub folders:

- *Tender Documentation* – this is a pristine copy of all of the RFT from the website and will include addendum as they are posted. These documents are kept in their original format and it is recommended that you add a copy of the main tender page from the organisation's site or tender portal.
- *Research* – this is a place to store any research relevant to the tender. The research remains on hand for reference and for citation, if required in the tender. There is nothing worse than knowing you

found a fabulous quote and have lost the link.

- *Drafts* – this is a place to put any working document. It includes later versions of drafts used for editing and proofing documents as you are working through the tender process.

- *OA Pipeline* - all documents relating to the OA including all decisions for go/no-go.

- *Project Management Internal* – this will include your project team management subfolders and any internal requirements along with the documents to support the internal project management process.

- *Project Management Tender* – this is a place to place procurement plans, project plans, risk assessments, etc., that are part of, and required in, the development of the tender.

- *Budgets* – a place to put any budgets and work in progress.

- *Correspondence* - a place to copy your emails relevant to the tender.

- *Legal* – depending on your business and the tender itself, there may be a contract that you can negotiate including any areas that you wish to change in the contract, if you are successful. Any contract in the RFT should be copied and placed in here and any correspondence with your legal department again should go within this folder.

- *Project/Review Teams* – this is an area for placing membership information, meeting notes and any communication with your project/review team.

- *Ready for Submission* – this folder is used for a copy of the final application/bid or the final word document for input into the online portal. I will explain more on this later. For now, this is one folder where you must have control limited to only people involved with the submission. It is a place to input the final submission and to hold other documents that are required pending the submission date.

- *Submitted* – this is a folder where the final submitted documents are placed, the proof of submission, and the documents that were provided to the organisation.

Below is an example of the folder tree I use for my

tender applications.

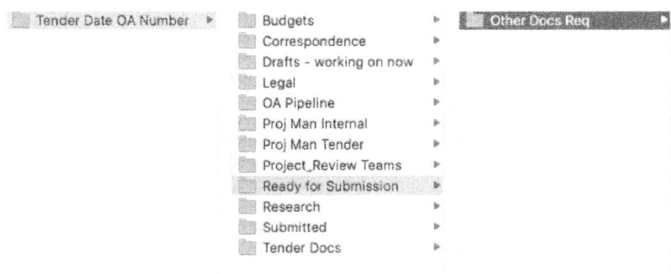

Folder Snapshot Example

Note: if you are working in a team of tender writers, it is worth setting up a consistent file tree that all tender writers work to. This ensures that anyone could go into the tender files and know exactly where to locate documents. It may be that someone has to take over your process. The more consistency you have in this administrative process, the easier it is for other people to pick up and understand where you are. Equally, you may have to pick up someone else's work.

Ensure the tender folder and subfolders are backed up to either your internal backup or a cloud backup environment. I use Dropbox or Office 365 as

I can access the documents anywhere. It negates the stress of lost documents, remote access and unforeseen circumstances such as power outages.

Set up file sharing with others involved in the process and manage that access. Do not be afraid to give some people restricted access. You are managing this process and you do not want the files within the *Ready for Submission* folder to be open to everyone in the team. That is not to say you do not trust them, but it is a way to control the information flow. If someone were to make an error, not understanding your process, it could significantly impact the quality of the application/bid document.

Secondly, with the folders in place it is time to download the tender documents into the *Tender Document* folder.

To download the RFT, you will need to have a registered account. This ensures that you are kept up-to-date with all the consequential documentation issued as a result of the ongoing tender process and includes addendum notified throughout the tender's question period. Addendum tend to come out relating to any changes to the RFT and will include questions from all parties involved in the tender process. These are answered in a global way so that everyone is advised of the information in one go.

Make a copy of the tender application document

into the *Drafts* folder. Change the name of the draft, per your organisational naming conventions and make it clear it is a draft and also date it. In some cases, the application is via data entry into an online portal. If this is the case create a draft working document with the questions and word count from the online portal. You may choose to do this anyway, as it does work well for adding notes such as who a question has been allocated to.

All drafts are kept in the *Drafts* folder. I am sure you will develop your own way of managing the drafts. You can save a new version as you add in new significant information. This ensures that you have older versions to refer to, but more importantly, it marks the progression of the writing and gives a visual of who has added what information or been consulted.

Copy the tender application or the main word document into the *Ready for Submission* folder. Again, per your organisational naming conventions, name this document and add 'final pre-submission'. This document holds only the final approved text in readiness for editing and final reviews. At this point, I do add the organisational information to the document. It helps me to get a global view of the document and note any additional information required. Quite often, there will be internal checklists in here that you can add to your tender checklist of required documents to source in readiness for submission.

Under the *Ready for Submission* folder set up an *other documents* subfolder. This is where you can keep your checklist of required documents and copies of the documents required.

In preparation to tender, you will have set up your OA pipeline. Define your approval process and download decision tool templates into the OA Pipeline and update your organisational database.

With the administration in place, it is now time to read through the tender documents and see what is required. I am a little older perhaps and because of that, recommend a print version of all the documentation. I know some people will be happy to work online and through the various computer hardware options. It is really your choice and preference and no way is better than the other. However, spend some time to get away from the screen.

CHECKLIST

- Have you set up the tender file tree?
- Have you made an organisation decision to template this process?
- Have you backed the files up to a secure or cloud source?
- Have you decided on the access to the files and granted permissions?
- Have you registered and downloaded the tender documents and set up the drafts in their correct folder?
- Have you added the organisational information to the ready for submission document and created the *other documents* checklist?

- Have you updated the OA Pipeline database and downloaded the decision tool?
- Have you read through the tender documents?

ORGANISATIONAL FIT TO TENDER

If you are fortunate, your business will have developed an OA tool and an OA Team to assess it. The OA process provides key areas for consideration backed up with a team who can take responsibility for decision making by assessing the tenders impact on the business. As a writer, it provides a consistent review process and sanctioning for going forward to tender or not. It is known in the tender environment as the go/no-go decision.

With or without the tool, there are clear areas for consideration. You can use the information below to assist with your assessment or by consideration of the process, to develop an OA tool specific to your business. This list is just a start to the process and covers the generic areas. As a business, there will be individual nuances to add.

The OA is the time to ask whether it is viable for your business to tender for this work. Is it worth your investment to tender, based on the potential of the award and the chances of success against the known competition? Here are the more pertinent questions to ask:

Is This the Right Tender?

Eligibility

By this point in the process, you will have pre-filled your organisational information into the main application. You will have assessed the application/bid questions and the requirements as a whole. Clear gaps in your business eligibility will be evident. Some will deem you ineligible to tender and will create a no-go at this stage. The surmountable gaps can be highlighted and costed in terms of staff and compliance to meet the requirements.

Structure

Organisations are clear on who may tender to

them. Calls for submissions from charities or not-for-profits will not suit a for-profit business. Business registration or corporate structure type may not be defined but implied. If you are a sole trader business, a one-person entity, then a National tender is going to be a stretch. What are they looking for? Can your business structure meet the needs?

Other Eligibility Requirements

Other eligibility requirements include the level of insurance. If the insurance requirements are for liability of $20 million and you only have $10 million, your business can make adjustments to meet the requirements. Required compliance or standards can be set by the organisation. Do you meet that requirement? If not, can you meet the standard with ease? Or is it a six-month process and out of the realms of possibility in the time until the tender closes for applications/bids?

Business Fit

The tender documents will state the project to be undertaken. If for example, they are looking for O-rings for an aircraft service and you deliver mental health services...well you do not fit. That is a simplistic example and it may be harder to assess. Your business has an overarching aim. You have a mission statement and a business plan and therefore, clear boundaries to your work activity. Does this tender fit those aspirations? Do you have the solutions to the RFT's needs, as in, do you have what they want or is it something that is a stretch for your business? Is there an obvious win theme for you within this tender? Can you see the way in which this tender is right for your business?

Is This Suitable for the Business?

Viability

During this part of the process, remember that you have business needs, including expectations to pay your creditors, overheads and staff. It is entirely acceptable to make a profit from a tender or, in the not-for-profit world, at least break even. Is there a clear profit to be made? If there is not, then it is not worth the effort to tender and have an award leading you directly to financial stress and potential for bankruptcy. Some tenders will offer fixed term activity pricing. They are telling you what they can afford to pay and not what you can afford to do it for. Now, is this viable over the longer term? A fixed term now will still require the ability to claim for yearly cost of living increases to your costs and wage awards at the very least. Is there mention of additional information in relation to the budget? Highlight them and report them as part of your OA. Flag these at this stage and present them to the OA Team.

Social Clauses

Social Clauses prioritise social needs in the community and can include employment initiatives, social enterprise, environmental and similar requirements within the scope of the RFT. Social clauses are becoming more common in the public organisation's tendering process and there is a movement to ensure they are included as part of organisations' procurement standard terms. Does the tender ask you to align to your community and social clauses? This is more common where, especially government departments, are looking to address their social issues and community responsibility within their procurement process. This relates to buying locally, employing locally, employing staff who are furthest from the employment opportunities. As a corporately responsible business, it is probably important to you too. It is also a good point to note for your win theme.

Risk Assessment

No project is without risks and every tender brings the opportunity for a new risk assessment and the development of mitigation strategies. This is a separate process and at this point, it is your role to highlight the obvious ones in the tender for the OA Team. You may be responsible for the risk assessment process, but remember this is not the time to invest in it fully. Because, if the decision is a no-go, you would have wasted hours that were not required. Always note that a risk assessment will be required if the tender is a go. For now, check and review what is expected under the tender. State the risks, offer some idea of possible mitigation and costs.

Budget Implications

I cannot stress this highly enough, budgets are the realm of a suitably qualified accountant. They have the skills to identify the budget implications. At this stage, it is your job to identify key areas of concern. Check whether there are additional costs involved such as new staff, new premises, additional software needs or other assets both internally and externally. Factor in a rough guide to the hours you will need to write the application/bid and the team you will need to support you in preparing the tender, including their costs. What staff, premises and other assets or peripherals are required? Factor in what it is going to cost you if you have to exit staff and close out contracts. If the lease for premises is for longer than the tender, highlight this as an issue for the OA Team.

Legal

Unless you are a lawyer, seek professional legal advice. Patents, commercial confidence and contracts will need to be protected and highlighted. These areas are clearly ones for the legal team to review and to consider viability under tender. It is your job to identify some early facts for the OA Team to consider. Eventually you will need a legal review of that contract to assess whether it is worth going for the tender. State that in your assessment every time.

Quality

There will be an element of quality assurance and management required in every tender. Some may be process-driven while some will require your business to meet quality standards. Do you meet the quality assurance elements of the tender? Does the organisation require industry-required certification such as an ISO? What is the impact to the business of managing that? By reviewing these questions, you will have some understanding of whether the activity is achievable in the longer term.

Staff

The impact of a tender on the staff is in relation to the application/bid, the impact of new activity and the need for employing more staff. Consider your current employees. Do they have the skills and qualifications required to carry out work under the tender and a subsequent award? What might it cost to up-skill them and keep them current over the term of the award? Will you need to recruit more staff for the award period? What would the contracts look like? What costs might be incurred in closing contracts at the end of the award? Is there a requirement to meet a certain pay level under the RFT or to employ staff with certain employment benefits? Consider their welfare and ensure your expectations of their capacity are valid to maintain their ongoing well-being. Seek your human resource support and always ask that they review this, if you get a *go* decision.

Assets

Tender awards have the potential to create expansion in your activity. Administration centres, delivery areas and production all take up space. Do you have the required space to meet the tender? Will you require new premises, new equipment or lease/hire arrangements to meet the activity you are tendering for? Can you obtain a lease/hire for the period of the tender or will you have unused capacity at the end?

Procurement

With all activity comes the need for your business to procure items for the tender. Procurement plans will need to be considered and the impact of new contracts identified. Are there issues you foresee from the RFT? Are there requirements to procure in a certain way or from certain types of supplier?

Time to Tender

Tendering takes time. It will impact on the tender team and take them away from their current roles and activity. Realistically, do you have the time to tender? This is the time to review the impact of planning, staff time and the energy they have to commit to the process. Get rough timelines and review the impact on their current workflow. Seek some clarification in coordinating the requirements, contributors and the required teams. It may be that you do not have time to tender on this occasion. The time between the open and close dates may be too short or it just might be a busy time for your current business activity and would negatively impact the current customer base.

Ability to Deliver the Outcomes

Once you have ascertained the ability to proceed to tender, you will need to assess whether you have the capacity to deliver the outcomes expected under the tender. What has your past performance been in relation to this type of tender or this type of instant growth in your business's workload? Have you achieved your goals? Did you have the resources and staff? Did you notice a high turnover in staff because of, perhaps, overwork? These areas are pivotal to assess at this stage. Keeping your business healthy in the tender process and beyond is a no-brainer. Considerations now, and mitigation of your process, will ensure your business has the energy to keep going into the future.

Competitive Edge

Where does your business stand out from the applicant pool, as in, how successful will you be with this tender? What is your value proposition? Your corporate differentiation? Your proposal strategy? What is the win theme for this tender?

Those in the OA Team will want your opinion on the chances of winning the tender. They want to know whether it is worth the investment of staff time and resources to prepare a tender and what they can expect to gain from it.

With your preparations for the OA assessment process, you will develop an overview and a robust understanding of the implications of submitting a tender. You will have a strength-based decision tool to take through to your OA pipeline for their review. You can give an honest appraisal of the tender. If the OA Team choose to go forward, even if you have highlighted some concerns, you have done your job. And your job is to remain vigilant to the issues, open to the opportunities and to maintain a conversation with those in the OA Team.

Your last job is to note the OA Team's comments and their decision. Keep this information in your *OA Pipeline* folder.

CHECKLIST

- Have you developed an OA Tool?
- Have you assessed whether this is the right tender for your business in terms of structure, eligibility and business fit?
- Have you assessed the tender in relation to viability, social clauses, risks, budget, legal, quality, staff, assets, procurements, time to tender, ability to deliver outcomes, and competitive edge?
- Have you developed an honest appraisal of the tender for the OA Team?
- Have you communicated it and set in place plans for future reviews, if required?
- Have you noted their responses to the OA

tool and their decision on the OA Pipeline database?

- Have you updated the files to your *OA Pipeline* folder?

RESEARCH: WHAT ARE THEY LOOKING FOR IN YOUR PROPOSAL

With the *go* decision in place, it is time to start the research **for the writing** of the application/bid. When researching the tender at this early stage in the process, you are really looking to see where there are gaps in your research and then where more extensive research will be required. You will have a wider project team and they will have areas of research relevant to their area of expertise. For now, we will concentrate on the aspects, you as a writer will focus on. It is recommended that you set the research into two stages: planning and the actual deep research.

Stage One - Planning the Research

Research is an area of the tendering process where you can really lose time, and in fact, waste a great deal of time. It is easy to go off on a tangent and to become interested in the work you are doing. With planning, you can identify the key questions your research needs to answer or the scope and the time and hours allocated to the task.

With reference to the RFT documents, map the areas requiring research. Look for key words such as evidence, need, identify and similar. Understand their impact on the RFT and the application/bid. Are they guiding you to targeted demographic data, comparative analysis, innovative research, etc.?

Identify the research the organisation accepts as current, authoritative and persuasive. If your business is in the international market place, your research pool could extend to a similar demographic. Examine the organisation's own documentation and gauge whether they have preferred research to use or even specific documents with acceptable research contained within.

Treat the Internet with caution. The Internet is full of information but, is it acceptable as research in respect of your tender? Is it peer reviewed and is it fact or opinion?

Consider your own business's research. Has it been provided in a research environment? Does the research have standing in the academic field? Is it valuable, in that, is it feedback from your customers and has it been collated in a standardised and ethical manner?

What is clear is, the research you need to undertake will be dictated by the RFT. Research will also help you with aligning your tender to the organisation to meet their: needs, corporate desires, and strategic vision.

Stage Two - Deep Research

Research for the tender is about information gathering and evidencing your statements. It is also about your competition and win themes.

Information Gathering

If you have prepared for the tender process, you will have some information in your generic research folders to start this process. You will have started to gain an understanding of the business environment and the areas where you want to gain more information. Spread out your research to find common themes and to identify research sites to use.

Evidence

Find hard data sources to use to answer your earlier questions. Your country will have a statistical division or bureau of statistics. They collect and analyse data sets and provide reports on a multitude of research terms. Contact them if you seek a particular data set. If they do not have it, they will have a good idea of where to go to find it. Utilise industry and academic sources relevant to your business.

Seek out quotations to use within respected sources and highlight them for quick reference. Save the useful ones to you *Research* folder and do not forget to find a way to manage citations so that you have them on hand if required.

The Competition

Competitive Intelligence is the process of checking out the competition. It is the legal and ethical way of checking out the competition by examining their information in the public domain. It is important to point out that research of your competitors is pivotal in the tender process. Understanding what they offer, the price they are likely to charge, their profit margins, their innovations, their processes, and their scale, i.e., overhead costs, as well as the customer reviews, will give you a greater understanding of the differentiators to your business. These differentiators will be your point of difference in your application/bid and will point you in the right direction for the win themes you follow as you progress the application.

The Tendering Organisation

The intelligence gathering extends to the organisation. Understand where the procurement fits in their overall business activity, their budget and their likely costings. Research their corporate responsibility, environmental perspective, vision and mission statements to understand them as an entity.

Win Themes

Win themes are the overarching features and benefits that dictate the point of view of the tender. There may be one or two themes that you will use and they focus on the key issue the organisation needs addressed from the RFT. Your win themes tend to be around costs, risk, the product or service offered or the level of innovation your application/bid offers. By this stage in your research, you will have a good understanding of which one to go with. If you are in doubt, look at the tenders they have awarded in the past and review the possible themes that would apply. It is an unknown, but it is also a place where you can make a judgement call.

Do not sit in isolation with the research. Check with your colleagues, especially the experts in your business to challenge your theories and add value to your research.

CHECKLIST

- Have you got a plan for your research in terms of time and scope?
- Have you undertaken the research?
- Is it saved into your *Research* folder and do you have the citations on hand, if required?

RESEARCH: YOUR AUDIENCE

The audience, when you write, will be one of the most challenging aspects of your role. I would love to tell you that everyone will read the RFT and will understand what the organisation is looking for, what they expect and how you must craft the response to meet the expectations. However, the reality is, they do not.

For your internal teams, this can be a hard concept, as people tend to have different viewpoints of who they are writing to. Some are so wrapped up in their specific area and creative style that it feels contrary and wrong to write in the way determined by the application/bid process. Dependant on their viewpoint, they will need some support to gain an understanding.

At this stage, remember it is your job to understand the tender expectations, communicate them to your peers, teams, managers and the signatory while at the same time remaining consistent in that message. Look for an assessment guide within the RFT. This document is a matrix of what the organisation is looking for in each question, the weighting they award to each question and the overall score. It may also state how they plan to manage the scoring mechanism and who will form the panel of assessors. Note the questions that earn a higher score, deserve stronger responses. See whether they are given more space in the response document or whether they require a concise, factual and targeted response.

Aim to get your management team involved in defining this for the team at an early stage. The management team's direction and support will ensure everyone works the same way. It will challenge some people and the person with that view may be part of the management team.

Gather the team. State the obvious - The audience for a tender will always be those people at the tendering organisation who are assessing the tender.

Brief the team on the tender document and provide the team with copies of the document. Ask them to work with you to define the assessor panel as an audience, understand what might be their expectations of the tender responses, the technical language you can use and what the assessor panel would be looking for in allocating scores. Confront your own stereotypes and seek to reach a consensus as to the audience.

This way, the team will work together writing to the same audience and the message will integrate the team's skills and writing strengths to deliver a strong win theme.

CHECKLIST

- Have you got a clear understanding of the potential audience for the tender?
- Have you briefed your team and sought consensus as to the way to write to that audience?

RESEARCH: THE SOFTWARE NEEDS

In this chapter, it is important to assess the RFT to see what is required to apply and submit your application early on in the tender writing process, in relation to the tender software requirements.

Within the documentation, there will be clarification to determine whether the submission method is by an online portal, via email or in a physical format.

Website Portal

If the submission method is via an online portal, there will be a hyperlink to the site. An instruction guide and a contact link to an IT specialist will be provided within the documentation or on the portal page. These are for you, should you encounter any issues.

Read the user documentation and ensure there is compatibility between your hardware/software and the organisation's. Some organisations are using old versions of software. Some have not written their programs to fully incorporate the transition from Apple to Windows or vice-versa. It is recommended that you test the system out early on to identify incompatibility and have time to resolve any glitches. Another issue is that at the time of submission, more information is being uploaded. It can freeze the portal. Allow yourself time to submit and plan to submit at least a day early.

Online applications/bids can be problematic. Some do not have the ability to spell-check. Others set a character or word limit. These can be frustrating, so let me explain.

Copy out the questions into a word document. Note the word limits and any additional info. In essence, transcribe the online application/bid to something you can work with. This allows entry of heaps of information, notes, multiple drafts and all of the elements that lead to the finished product. Some online forms fail to mirror the character count of your word processing software. You may have exactly the character count required off line. Somewhere between the act of copying out of your word-processing software and pasting into the portal, a number of characters are added in, or have failed to be counted, and that pristine text you have toiled over will not fit into the text box. Save yourself the stress and test this out early. Better still, as you finish sections enter them in.

Email

Email is not as common as online or physical lodgement but it deserves discussion. Email has some unique potential for issues. Do check the software versions the organisation can accept and the size of the files they can receive on their server. Allow time for any bounce backs and do not rest until you have a proof of receipt from the organisation.

Physical Lodgement

Some organisations will ask for the tender in hard copies. They will be clear in the manner of presentation, the number of copies and if there is a requirement for an e-version. Common requests are for the application/bid to be in triplicate.

If you have a hard copy submission you will need to understand whether the proof of posting relates to the date posted or the date it arrives. Consider whether you may want to utilise printers for the physical print and couriers for delivery. Order the printer and courier time ahead as many have a backlog of work. Like the other submission formats, plan for a no-stress submission in terms of time allowed for the parties involved.

The most important message from this chapter is to plan for the fact that in the days leading up to the submission date, the Internet will freeze, the printer will jam and the technician will not be available for 24 hours, there will be a power outage, or some other joyous event will happen to stand between you and successful submission. If you plan for this event and plan to submit earlier than the tender close time, the chances of this happening seem to reduce. It is always better to aim to submit a day or two earlier than the submission date as tenders have a firm close. This means if the time of submission lapses as you are halfway through entering your tender, they will close you out and will not accept your application/bid. I am yet to find any tender process that has any flexibility around the close time even if there are major issues around the submission. The reason for this is, the organisations have a fair and equitable procurement process. So, to waiver these timelines for poor planning would be directly in conflict with that.

CHECKLIST

- Have you ascertained the method of submission for the application/bid?
- Have you read the supporting documentation?
- Have you noted the IT contact details?
- Have you factored in time to submit the application/bid reducing stress on all parties?

Website Portal

- Does your hardware/software cause any issues with the organisation?

- Have you prepared a way to work in draft?
- Have you checked whether the online portal recognised the word count of your draft software?

Email

- Have you checked the software and file size requirements of the organisation?
- Have you noted the need for a receipt?

Physical Lodgement

- Have you determined the date of posting to ensure delivery by the close date?
- Have you planned for printing and courier services, if required?

PLANNING: PROJECT TIMELINES FOR THE TENDER PROCESS

Project-managing the writing of the tender application/bid and submitting it, is a project in itself. It will require the management of your time, your project team and the process of tracking the tender from its identification to its submission and beyond.

For this process, like any project management process, you will need to work backwards in the planning process. As always, the primary date is the date of submission (including the time of day stipulated). The reason for setting this as a primary date, is it is the one thing that is fixed and every activity must work towards achieving it.

Working backwards may seem a weird and complex way of working. However, it gives you certainty and urgency in relation to the time you have available. Always factor in more time than you expect to undertake on each activity, as time will always work against you. We always think we can achieve things quicker than we actually do. Issues come up, deadlines get pushed and activity is delayed. In addition, many people working on tender team are time-poor, as they will be working on the application/bid in conjunction with their normal working routine.

In the project timeline planning, you are planning for you and your team. Rigorous project management will deliver a quality application/bid. It will create urgency in those around you and give you the ability to manage their expectations and time commitment.

Depending on your business, timelines will vary in direct correlation to the level of complexity of the tender. It will also directly correlate to the size of your business and the level of red tape and bureaucracy you may have to wade through to achieve your outcomes. The project management process is a stepped approach to the writing. It will allow you to monitor your progress in real time and provide a reporting structure to those you are accountable to.

With a tender, the project management process will probably be managed through a software package. This may be something as simple as Microsoft Excel or a more complex project management software utilised by your business. Ensure that whatever you use, allows you to track the activity and gives you the project status in real-time. This will give you a good level of accountability.

However good your project management tools are, there is still the requirement for you to allocate time to writing and to encourage members of your team to commit to the project. These management tools are pivotal to the project's success and will engender the team as well as provide your management with the level of accountability and comfort in knowing the tender is moving along the right pace.

Here is an example of the activities in the order that is recommended to plan them into a tender timeline.

- Ergonomics, health and safety, and insurance identified
- Identify Tender
- Set up administration
- Entry into OA Pipeline database and book meeting for the go/no-go
- Appraise tender per OA Tool and complete tender document checklist
- Complete research
- Complete tender management plan

- OA meeting and subsequent note of decision in opportunity pipeline database for go/no –go
- Book kick-off meetings and schedule critical milestones for review
- Set planning timelines both internal and external
- Map milestones
- Complete project scheduling
- Complete project management plan timelines (internal)
- Identify project team and book team meetings
- Complete tender research
- Commence project plan
- Complete first project management group and subsequent meetings into project management plan
- Book time slots for writing staff, editing team and formal sign off
- Identify additional documents
- Check additional documents for validity and save
- Complete project research
- Identify referees and gain support
- Develop and deliver endorsed project plan
- Complete application/bid writing

- Allocate space to step away from application
- Complete editing and proofing
- Create briefing document for authorised signatory
- Formal sign off by authorised signatory – make this two days before submission date at a minimum
- Planned date of submission
- Formal date of submission
- Update OA database
- Complete post tender activity including review meeting

With the project timelines scheduled, it is time to book times with members of the project, review and editing team as well as the signatory.

CHECKLIST

- Have you got the *go* to tender?
- Have you scheduled project timelines for internal project plan?
- Have you booked the relevant time slots with those involved in the process?

PLANNING: THE PROJECT PLAN

Project planning is at the heart of the tender process. It is an intrinsic step in the development of the project and important for you, as a writer, to understand each facet of the project to develop your voice in the application/bid narrative and overall win theme. Done right, it will give you the information to respond to the tender and the evidence base from which to work to. It will include all relevant aspects of the project and it will be your job as the tender writer to bring any tender specific requirements to the project team so they are included in the project plan.

The project team brings expertise. Their input and experience is invaluable to the project plan in terms of specification, production, costing, timelines and specialist expertise. Some will have been through the tender writing process and can offer you an opportunity for mentoring and ongoing support. By consensus, the project team can assist with the identification of the win theme(s) and the probable expectations of the organisation in terms of the tender itself.

The size of your team and the number of experts will vary depending on the size of your business. You may be leading this team or be a component part of it. Either way, as a writer, you will need to clearly state your needs as part of the project team and ensure the tender writing project plan is communicated and understood by all parties within the team.

For bigger businesses, there will be an established project management framework and people trained in using it. You may have an established template for project planning or an off-the-shelf product or service ready to be adapted in terms of delivery and costing.

If you do not have a project plan template in place, you will need to develop a new project plan.

The way you develop the plan will depend on your team. Some will meet physically, others virtually. Some will be led by you and others by a team leader. As the tender writer, you need to have a clear understanding of the project. Ask the team leader in conjunction with the project team to produce a one page/one whiteboard visual of the project. This is the overarching theme and each member can be directed to their part in the project and also visualise the project as a whole.

Your business may develop a mission statement and project name at this stage.

The project plan is essential to the tender process. Depending on the complexity, the plan may be a matter of a number of pages to a complex document. Invest time in this development process. It will negate issues, if the tender is awarded, and will make the writing easier.

The list below contains some of the main headings recommended that you use in project planning, in no particular order, as you will need to align these to your business and adapt it to your planned activity.

The plan includes:

- The name of the project
- The start and end date
- Project Manager
- An executive summary - write this last
- Organisational capability in this area
- Strategic impact
- Approvals process
- Partners/referees/testimonials

- Project staff contact details
- Project staff job descriptions and resumes
- Planned staff team including and a clear picture of their work hours, their reporting structure and their educational qualifications/job descriptions
- The aims and objectives of the project
- The need for the project, including competition analysis of potential competitors in the tender process
- Proposal management process
- The research and the gaps in research
- Target groups, if relevant, including ages, gender, demographics, and the proposed number you will target
- Target group outcomes and benefits
- Activity and timeline of the project
- Risk assessments and management
- Deadlines
- Scheduling before, during and after tender submission
- Entry and monitoring for tracking protocols for critical milestones
- Measurement and evaluation
- Quality
- The project management team members, contact details

- Procurement plans internal
- Procurement plans external - including printers, couriers
- Tender specific procurement plans and will include directions such as, no sub-contracts issued until tender in place
- External expert reviewers such as legal, accountants
- Additional resources required, including premises, information and communications technology
- Research and development activities
- Editing and proofing team
- Production plans
- Service delivery plans
- Complaints procedures
- Compliance
- Relevant policies and processes such as finance for acquittal, and Human Resources for recruitment and screening
- Advertising and marketing including co-branding, if required
- Internal literature to support this project such as annual reports, track- record, etc.
- Additional anticipated costs to meet funder requirements, such as insurance
- Budgets and models

- Conflict management process
- Coordination of team and expectation in terms of tender responses and actions
- Project Management Team Meeting schedules agreement
- Milestone map and achievements
- Exit strategies
- Project plan approvals process

Any subsequent changes to the plan due to, for example, budget constraints, can be factored in and activity scaled up or down before you write. It is a *live* document, and everyone can focus on their individual parts in the project. By the writing stage, the changes will be minimised.

Always save the project plan and any amendments into your relevant subfolder under the *Project Management Internal* folder.

CHECKLIST

- Have you got a one page overview of the project?
- Do you understand your role in the project?
- Has your project team developed a full project plan?
- Have you saved the documents to the relevant subfolder under the *Project Management Internal* folder?

PLANNING: THE PROJECT PLAN REVIEW

A robust project plan is pivotal to tender writing. The plan is not final until it has been endorsed by the project team and the management of your business. You will need to develop a process to endorse it and to maintain an ongoing approval process to give it legitimacy over the longer term.

The project plan review demands each of the main project team has had an opportunity to input into the plan, review it as a finished document and to have approved its content. This is especially so with professional and expert members of your team or your business. These include, but are not limited to, your legal team who will review the tender contracts and their impact on the project, financial experts in relation to the budget and financial modelling and those involved in the product or service including timelines and estimations.

Approvals need to be either a physical initial on the project plan itself or via an alternative way. This may be an email or similar detailing approval. Either way, ensure that this is saved into your *Project Management Internal* subfolder and kept for future reference. This protects you where someone denies their approval of a stage of the writing or there is an issue with an element of the plan.

If you plan to submit your project plan in the future as an appendix to the tender, treat is as a professional document. Do not be afraid to add in design features to make it more aesthetically pleasing and follow your branding guidelines. The more professional your submitted documents are, the more professional your application/bid will be perceived.

Save your final plan to your *Project Management Internal* subfolder.

With all of this information consolidated into one document and approved, you are ready to map it to the tender documents and find your individual voice to convert it into your persuasive writing style/voice to underpin the win theme.

CHECKLIST

- Have you set up a formal approval process for the project plan?
- Have the team and relevant managers endorsed the document?
- Have you saved their approvals and the plan to your project folders?
- If the plan is to be submitted as an appendix, have you prepared a professional document?
- Have you saved the plan to your *Project Management Internal* subfolder?

PLANNING: BUDGETS

In relation to budgets, I am not a financial expert nor a trained accountant. For this reason, the actual budget for the tender will fall within the scope of the project plan. This chapter is for you to consider value added options, to strengthen your budget and improve your bottom line profit and provides you with some strategies you can use to improve cost effectiveness and linkage to other funding streams.

At all times, keep in mind that your budget is a plan for success and a means to ensure your project is a viable and thriving opportunity for your business. If you are looking for an award from the tender to keep your business viable, consider whether this is the right option for you.

If your business is finding it tough, is it really more work you need? Or is it that you need to improve your costings? Your process? You have to have a viable business and a viable project/product/service to enter into the tendering process. Why? Because your competition will have. Expect that their track record on delivering tenders is based on delivering quality outcomes on time and within budget.

Use Professionals

Your application/bid is reliant on sound financial advice and, in all cases, seek either your internal financial team or the services of an accountant. These experts will ensure all of your costs are factored in and the costs match the project management plan's project activity. They can model your budget for impact to your business in its widest sense and allow for key considerations such as exit strategies, which will be discussed later. They will also highlight if it is viable to proceed to tender. The go/no-go is not limited to the initial OA assessment. It may be that as you unpack the tender documents as a team, it is not worth the investment. That said, it is time to look at improving the budget.

Cost Savings

There are always opportunities to make some cost savings for your business. They may come in the form of Government Initiatives, costings relating to the whole of business, other income streams and tax.

Government Initiatives

Government initiatives are available in some areas. They tend to follow the current political will to drive gross domestic product, social and community needs. These include environmental initiatives for power use and the use of renewables, manufacturing assessment and production line improvements, export, innovation and research. They extend to initiatives to strengthen the workforce and to employ the long term unemployed and those suffering significant disadvantage due to their proximity to the labour market. These incentives are in the public domain and can be linked into via the Government portals relating to employment, unemployment and business.

Other Government Support

In addition to the fiscal initiatives, training and

development in the form of ongoing training, mentoring and the use of consultants is often advertised via governmental portals on an ongoing basis. Government may provide these initiatives free of charge or for a matched funded investment or at a reduced cost to your business. Check in with your local Chamber of Commerce or business department to link in with the opportunities.

There may be opportunities for research and development with your local educational institutions and quite often, these attract additional funding to support your partnership.

Whole of Business Considerations

The Premises

Sometimes there is the opportunity to gain incentives for your business from your local council in relation to premises costs. There may be incentives to move to the location in terms of a free period on the tenancy or a reduction in rates. Options are limited, but it is worth exploring this if you have the option to relocate. With any lease, ensure the cost is factored into the tender including costs associated with terms outside of your tender award period and thus outstanding at the end of the tender.

Internal Costings

Consider where you can add value to the tender whether it is by sharing some internal costs with your current activity or whether, by volume of work, you can create cost savings including utilising staff and resources to their full capacity.

Supply Chain

Review your supply chain and see where you can create cost savings. If you have a guaranteed income for a guaranteed length of time, you can secure better terms with your suppliers including deep discounting for your continued custom.

Modelling

Modelling allows you to test different scenarios to gain the best perspective for your business. Model different budget scenarios for your business activity and for the tender. By comparative analysis, you may find a more streamlined budget and extend your profit margin.

Value Adding

Value adding is the ability to make money from your current activity. It is another way to reduce budget costs and improve profit for your business. It may be that you can develop a training package for a particular service delivered by the tender and then sell it as part of your service offerings, or a similar duplication of your knowledge, service and production components during the tender and after the award has been completed.

Other Income Streams

Grants

Grants are available to business through your local, state and federal government departments. Make contact with them to see if they support elements of your business to encourage business growth, export, research and innovation. This is more applicable to the not-for-profit or social venture that may be able to access start-up funding to sustain the viability of their enterprise in the long term by use of the tendering process. Check with your country's business and social venture community for opportunities, as well as the government grant portals.

Tenders

In developing your processes for this tender, there is an opportunity to access more tenders and to have a strategic plan to maximise this revenue stream. The cost savings in central costs can be spread over multiple tenders thus increasing your cost effectiveness.

Tax

Ask for advice from your local tax office for the incentives they offer to business. It may be the ability to purchase and depreciate certain assets within a year to incentives to reduce payroll taxes within different states.

These are some ideas of how you might reflect on your budgeting and I am sure you will add more to them as you work through the process. Remember, it is always best to seek expert internal/external financial advice for tenders as they will have a robust understanding of the costing required, the modelling for future scenarios and initiatives that may assist you to ensure you have a strong profit margin across your business.

CHECKLIST

- Have you considered the cost savings and initiatives offered in your local area?
- Have you sought the advice of a financial expert/accountant to review them?

WRITING: STYLES

Writing Styles relate to understanding the requirements of the audience you are addressing or are
targeting, i.e., who is reading it, the format of the
document, the need for formal or informal responses,
mandated style guides and the assessor's perspective
and requirements and the way you can use that to
develop your writing style to produce a winning and
engaging response.

The Audience

As a tender writer, you need to personify the audience of the tender and create a fictitious character as
the one person you write to. This fictitious character
embodies the needs of the RFT and the organisation

who published it, the assessors and your business. By taking time to build this person in your mind, you will structure the application/bid in such a way as to maintain your win theme, your point of view of your response and your voice throughout the application/bid. It makes your writing process easier as, instead of trying to please a group of people, you are working with just one.

The Format

What does the fictitious character expect in terms of the way the document will be set out?

Refer first to the tender documents. They tend to mandate the font and size requirements to ensure every application/bid is uniform in their responses. They may detail a character limit or word limit for responses in the RFT or it may be a part of the application.

A recent tender I worked on did not have a word count. The organisation asked for the responses to be 'succinct', as the only guide. The application was in Microsoft Excel and the cell for the responses opened to a fixed size. This equated to a response of about 350 words. The organisation was contacted and they were happy for information to go beyond the cell to be added to an appendix in the text.

In this case, it was clear that the organisation was new to the tendering process having moved over from a grants environment only a few months before. I would hazard a guess that the intention was to follow the succinct direction in the tender documents to a 350-word count. This had not been communicated but implied in the size of the Excel cell size.

When there is uncertainty in the RFT and the response from the organisation is vague or their advice will weaken your response, it is a tough call for how you respond. Letting responses extend into an appendix stops the flow of the answer and weakens the win theme. In truth, many writers are keen to use more words to drive their argument home. Many assessors will tell you less is more. A well-written application will keep the responses tight and will still drive home a winning message. It is your call to make based on your research of the organisation.

One way to keep the responses succinct is by using visuals in the application/bid or by attaching other documents in appendices. The RFT does not always state whether appendices are allowed. Or, if it does, the appendices may be limited to specific documents such as, the requirement to substantiate your capacity and capabilities such as the inclusion of curriculum vitae, process mapping, budget information, insurance documentation, and, as in the case above, if they will allow you to extend the responses onto a separate document. If you are unsure, ask the organisation. Normally, they will have stated that you can ask questions up to a certain date and this is the time to really question these style issues to get a firm guideline for writing.

Formal or Informal Response

What does the fictitious character expect in terms of the way you speak to them? The tender writing style is, by default, formal and this is never more apparent than when your responses, or part of them, will form a part of the final contract. If this is the case, draft the response and run it past your legal experts. Some will provide you with an edited document or they will provide you with a block of legalese to use in this, and future, applications/bids. As the law changes in the blink of a 'stated case', never take the response as accurate for future tenders and always ask your legal team to ensure it is still current as per your generic review process.

By contrast to the formal approach, some former grant rounds have been transitioned to a tender process. In these RFTs, the organisation may maintain a requirement for an informal response. You can gauge this in some way by your interaction with the organisation or in your communication with them. You can also gain some insight in the way they ask their questions. For example, do they ask the questions in a personal or professional manner, i.e., what will 'your' business do? Or what will 'the' business do? In the two examples, 'your' or 'the' gives you a really honest appraisal of whether your response is in the informal first person, *we*, *our* or the formal third person, *the business*. If they are talking about your business, they are asking the questions in a personal way and it gives you the opportunity to write in the first person. First person responses are a better way to creative an emotive response in the reader.

Mandated Style Guides

Does this fictitious character have a published style guide? Due to the more formal approach of the tender writing process, your writing style in the tender environment is usually dictated within the RFT or by your business. If you are in doubt, the organisation's direction in the RFT is the writing style guide you use.

Examine the organisation's style guide and your business's internal style guide and branding restrictions to determine how you are going to write to answer the questions. Government departments will have their own style guides and they are available in bookshops or online to purchase. Sometimes it is easier to stick with the organisation's style guide, it is what they expect, it is how they view the world and, as far as a well-written proposal goes, it will meet their expectations. If you are unsure, ask the question of the organisation, as to what style guide has to be followed by your business. Do not be afraid to ask questions of them as many other people will be and this is what sparks ongoing addendum to be released throughout the open tender process. Keep yourself apprised of the ongoing published addendum as you write. The directions within the addendum could impact the ongoing writing process and never submit your application/bid before the close of questions. You could miss out on a direction that impacts your final application/bid.

You may find your own internal style guide is different in many ways. It may be a mandated document to follow by your business. If that is the case, it is an internal project team decision as to which way you, as the tender writer, approach the tender writing. Ask for the project team to make the decision, note it and save it to the *Internal Project Management>Project Team* subfolder.

The Assessors Perspective and Requirements

What is the fictitious character's role in the assessment of the application/bid? The impact of the assessment team on your writing style is also important. If you are tendering to rebuild a road, the chances are you will be writing to a pool of assessors whose expertise is in the engineering field. They, as assessors, will require your writing to be linear, factual, to the point and they will not be swayed by emotions. Conversely, if you are tendering to health organisation for the opportunity to offer service provision in their community, the assessors are more likely to have expertise in the health, social and community fields. They will understand the needs of their community and they will require an emotive element to the application/bid.

It may seem that writing for tenders is quite restrictive, but there is scope for you as a writer. You have control over the point of view, the story telling, the persuasive nature of the win theme, and the craft in your writing to utilise formatting in order to point the reader to your most salient points.

Remember, less is more. Write for impact. Edit back at every opportunity. You can see from the three sentences you have just read, they are short, to the point, and all in a few words. The more persuasive you want to be, the shorter the sentence, the shorter the information. Going back to the 350-word count example at the start of this chapter, you might say it is better to stick to the word count and scale back.

Write a bad draft to get the words on paper, then edit back to make your writing as succinct and professional as possible. Utilise acronyms to minimise text by adding them at the start of the document and then maintain their use throughout the document. The organisation may have their own too. You can always add in an acronym appendix to make the assessor's life easier.

At all times, you are writing for the assessor and their scoring matrix. Sometimes you will know what the scoring matrix is and how they are awarding points and for what questions. Make it easy for them to mark your work and to award the points in a progressive and linear way. Use graphics and diagrams, if they are allowed in the application/bid.

Make it easy for the assessor to test your argument. Understand, if there is a requirement for a research-intensive response, what the expectation is for citations or for commonly known information. Research-intensive responses tend to have a higher word limit to allow for longer citations. If they do not, again ask the question of the organisation for clarification.

Understanding your assessor and writing to their

preference, will strengthen your application/bid. Your research and active questioning of the organisation will yield some certainty to the writing style.

In all cases, remember the assessor is a professional customer. They want to see your business on the page. They want to see quality, excellence, a good command of language and a persuasive argument for why they should award you the tender.

Now you have worked through this chapter, you will see your fictitious person is predominantly the assessor.

CHECKLIST

- Have you determined whether there is a firm style guide to follow?
- Have you gathered the nuances within the tendering documentation and asked further questions to clarify your writing style?
- Have you researched the potential expectations of the assessor and planned your writing to them and their preferred writing style?
- Have you sought endorsement from your project team, noted their decision and saved it to the *Project Team folder*?

WRITING: ANSWERING THE QUESTIONS

This chapter is separated into three parts. Preparing to write, the writing and the final document. It does not provide you with sample answers. The reason is that a tender needs to be owned by your business. The words written in response deserve to be unique, targeted to your win theme and in your voice and style.

Preparing to Write

The following information relates to the assessed questions in your draft '**document**'. It is also presumed that you have developed a project plan, a budget and a project timeline in preparation to respond.

With the RFT and the questions, map the questions for the information you feel needs to go in each response. Put in dot point, rough notes and even a planned flow for your future writing's win theme.

Once completed, it is time to review the document as a whole.

- Are there places where your responses overlap?
- Do you need to remove duplication as the answers fit better under one question than another?
- Does the information flow over the whole document?
- Have you mapped the project plan to the questions?
- Where are the gaps?
- Do you need more information?
- Have you highlighted areas for appendices to be added?
- Is there the potential for diagrams?
- Is there a place for the budget?
- Have you got the budget in the right format for entry?
- Are there cross reference points within to note?

- Does your win theme develop over the answers?
- Do you answer the questions?
- Have you added your research?
- Have you linked in the generic information?
- Have you allocated specialist areas to the wider writing team?
- Have you located areas for professional input and advice?
- Have you identified the main writer responsible for the main document?

At the end of the review you will have a skeleton of the proposed answers. Share your planned responses with the project team and ask for their input. As a team, drill down and assess whether the planned responses meet the needs of the assessor. Are the questions easy to follow? Is each answer building on the previous one to develop your win theme and provide a linear, well-researched application/bid?

By doing this as a project team, or at least as a writing team, you will all understand your role in the process. You will know how each element fits into the wider response and how each facet of the writing drives the overall win theme. You will have mapped the project plan and have the elements of it mapped to the questions.

You will also know where you may need to seek further clarification from the organisation. If you are unsure of the wording of a question, or if it is ambiguous, you thus have time to question the organisation.

Writing

The benefit of the time spent in planning is that your document has the information at hand, it is mapped, there is a clear plan of attack to the writing, a finalised flow for the answers is agreed and you are now ready for the writing phase. You do not need answers from an external source, as you have it already. Everyone involved in the writing is briefed, work has been allocated and it is time to work through the questions allotted to you from the document and to understand how you deal with your responses and what is expected of you, if you are managing the document as the main writer.

One of the greatest inventions for writers is the Nuance voice recognition software - Dragon. In some versions, there is the ability to dictate your work onto a voice recorder, save the file to your computer and transcribe it to text. It is something recommended for the draft stage only, as Dragon allows you to use a handheld voice recorder, your tablet phone or speak it directly onto the page. While it takes a bit of time to set up, if you are a 35-40 wpm typist, it returns that time in the speed you can get the words onto the page. Whether using voice dictation or typing, when writing the first draft of your response, write it badly. Get the words onto the page.

It is tempting at this point to consider using responses to a previous tender's questions and to just copy them and tweak them. Using your old work or someone else's work will change the flow of the words, it would change the feeling and embodiment of the writing and it will weaken your tender in most cases. By all means refer to it, update it and use it as some sort of platform to develop a new response in your own voice, in your own words, and in your own way.

Like the mapping exercise, the first draft gives you the structure of your response and the final document. From here you can review the overall document and start your three-stage editing process.

Stage 1: read it over as a complete question or document and see whether it answers the question, is written for the assessor, covers all of the points you wanted to and progresses your win theme. Be tough on yourself at this point. As you have written this work, ask someone else who has not had any input into your writing to see if they understand what you are trying to say and do. Note the changes.

Stage 2: Complete a full edit, and get it to a revised professional draft.

Stage 3: Read it aloud. Another part of the brain reviews what it hears and you will find new mistakes in the text. At this point you can make the final edits in readiness for the review team.

As you receive input on the questions from other writers and specialists, take their work through the three-stage process. Update Stage 1 to incorporate an extra step. When you are incorporating other people's work, it needs to match the voice of the main writer. You need to assess whether it feels out of place in language and flow. If it does, work with the specialist to determine a common ground for the responses. If it has to be written in that way, for example, if you have an engineering aspect and the writing is quite linear and to the point as it would be expected to be, then find a way to introduce it into the flow of the main document or go back and review the flow of the other questions to standardise the text.

Final Document

When you have the questions document at its final stage, it is time to ensure you have met the tender requirements in terms of the word/character count and fit in the application/bid document.

With the complete document, read it through as a final document, make any last edits and adjustments to the flow, check that the win theme builds to a persuasive argument and answers the questions for the aim of the tender. Save it as final draft in your *Drafts* folder.

CHECKLIST

- Have you saved your assessed questions' document to a separate draft file?
- Have you mapped the responses and linked it to your project plans?
- Have you allocated questions to specialist writers?
- Have you identified who the main writer is and who will maintain the central win themes and tender flow?
- Have you taken your response through the three-stage editing process?
- Have you taken responses from other writers through the same process?
- Have you assessed the final document?

- Have you saved the final document to your draft file?

REFERENCES

If the tender requires you to provide references, ensure that you choose the most relevant people to support your tender. It is tempting to use a friend or someone who you know will give you an absolutely positive review. But think again about that decision, as the status and stature of your reference will have an impact on your tender.

Think about the person or people who would be respected by the organisation. Consider whose advice they would seek as to your suitability. Would they benefit from knowing you are in a strong financial position such as the reference from your accountant? Or someone who has an understanding of your ability to provide services such as representative body? Or someone involved in your production line process who may have seen that your quality and excellence over time has impressed them, such as an external quality assessor?

Brief the referee on the tender process and what you plan to do. Ask them for their opinion on how they see you as a business and how that would reflect in a reference. Ensure they have a positive understanding of your capability, your current and future direction and business focus. Spend time with them and engage them along your business processes and timelines.

Let the referee know what to expect from the tender reference process, what they may be asked, and how that might look as far as a time commitment from them.

Keep the referee apprised of the tender process including when you plan to submit the application/bid, when the organisation might seek references, and what they will ask this person to contribute.

Ensure the referee's contact details are up-to-date, even if you have contacted them in the past couple of months. Have a conversation about where they might be around the time of the tender being submitted. Ask for an alternative way to contact them if they are out of the state or the country. If they have a time when they cannot be contacted, such as a holiday, note that, so you can respond to the organisation if they are chasing references at a later date. Seek an approved way to contact the referee and times they are happy to receive a call. The last thing you want to do is alienate your referee when they are volunteering their support of your tender.

It is important to maintain the relationship with the referee over time, so that you can seek their support at any time, and with subsequent tenders. Invite them to your events and keep them apprised of your achievements and new activities. By doing this, you ensure they are up-to-date on your business and you can rely on them for future references, if required.

CHECKLIST

- Have you identified referees who are suitable for the tender?
- Have you apprised the referee of the process?
- Have you got up-to-date contact information for the referee and alternative means to contact?
- Have you identified their availability?
- Have you set in place an ongoing channel to maintain the relationship over time?

OTHER DOCUMENTATION REQUIRED

The RFT documentation is specific about the other documentation the organisation requires to be submitted with the application/bid. This is normally eligibility type documentation and includes insurance, statutory compliance and organisational documentation such as business number, business registration date and type. It can include process mapping, staff resumes and similar documents.

It is your role to follow the RFT to the letter with the documentation you provide. Do not think you can add more to circumvent word counts, strengthen your tender writing or to strengthen your responses, unless you have spoken to the organisation and gained permission to add the additional information. Thinking you can add in reams and reams of additional information is not only disrespectful to the organisation's process, it could make your tender ineligible for not meeting the guidelines.

With any documentation you provide, ensure it is current. Insurance documentation is updated annually and it is easy to pick up the old certificate. If the insurance certificate is likely to run out pre-award, let the funder know that you are aware of that and add in information about continuing insurance beyond the date.

As part of the planning process, you have set yourself a checklist of the additional documentation you need to locate. Allocate it as a project activity in the project plan to actively secure it, and save it to your *Ready for Submission>Other Documents Required* folder. Ensure the file size is set to the smallest size to remain readable. That way you have the information ready to go in the best format for when you are ready to submit your application/bid. Keep your active checklist in the same *Ready for Submission>Other Documents Required* folder and add any additional information you find as you are developing the application/bid. This checklist not only takes the pressure off you to remember, it serves as a submission checklist too. It is all about removing the stress from the submission day.

If you have multiple attachments for the application/bid, it is worth putting together an appendix matrix and contents list. Brand it and design it to match your business's professional standing. Make it easy for the tender assessor to find and locate the documentation from an administrative perspective, as well as, within the tender document.

CHECKLIST

- Have you identified the other documents required under the RFT?
- Have you set up your checklist and planned activities to locate them?
- Are the documents in date?
- Have you saved them to the *Ready for Submission>Other Documents Required* folder in the best size and format to send?
- Have you developed an appendix matrix and contents list?

EDITING AND PROOFING

For any of you who have read my book, Grant Writing: A Simple, Clear and Concise Guide, you will know that editing and proofing are two of my particular peeves. Editing and proofing a document are such particular skills that I readily admit to using external editors when my work is going into the public domain.

As a writer, you do not see your own mistakes and a typo can come screaming off the page, smack you in the mouth and you still will not see where it is. After you have been staring at the words for so many days, the errors can become part of the imprint on your brain.

You can also be sensitive to feedback. It is your work, it is a part of you and it can feel personal when the feedback comes in. Accept that as fact and embrace the opportunity for feedback.

If you feel you have the editing and proofing skills required and can honestly say you can see your own mistakes, then, by all means, edit your own work. But, and there is a but, at least use a review team of peers who have not had any part in writing the tender documents to review it to check to see if that is the case.

Editing and proofing need a fresh set of eyes. In the tender writing process, you will set up a team of reviewers. The members of this team must have had no exposure to the writing itself. They will also be experts in their specialist area. You or your project team will choose them based on their role in the macro and micro editing and proofing stages of the application/bid.

Micro Reviewers: Stage One

These members are drawn from specialist areas to review component parts of the application/bid to ensure the document is factual. They may also extend their micro review to the whole document (macro) to ensure their element fits in with the flow of the document.

Macro Reviewers: Stage Two

These members are within the Management structure and will review the application/bid document on a whole-of-business basis. Their input relates to the flow of the document, the win theme and the business expectation as to the quality of the responses.

Micro Reviewers: Stage Three

These members are the branding experts, the administration team and those with a keen eye to the content on a line by line basis.

Macro Reviewers: Stage Four

These are the members of the review team who are the most senior managers. They will expect to see a finished product and may also be the signatory to the application/bid.

With the macro review team members, select them for their strengths, think how they add value and understanding to the tender process as a whole. If you have partners in the application/bid, ask them to review the project for the partnership elements and you are quite within your rights to ask for a non-disclosure agreement, approved by your legal team, to allow them access.

Select those in the management structure that are trusted by your signatory and consider internal professionals such as your legal and financial teams or externals, as required. In some cases, you can speak to the government officer or organisations who will review the application/bid document as it is being progressed. If you can get the government officer to assist you, they will add strength and value to your tender process.

The micro reviewers need to understand the application/bid as a final document. They may include graphic designers to review the aesthetics and others working towards the final document print.

Stage 1 of the editing and proofing can run alongside the development of the application/bid. It can happen as each question is finalised or at the end as a complete document.

Stage 2 and 3 require a final draft and the way you manage this is your individual choice but it is important to understand the issues that may arise.

Stage 4 is reserved for those who review the final document pre-submission.

Ideally, the draft application/bid document will move from one reviewer to the next to the next in a progressive and linear way. In that manner, the reviews build upon each other and you have chance to review the feedback before it moves on to the next person. The downside is that it needs to be a process increasing in hierarchy because as someone changes something, someone else may not like it and changes it again. It is easier if the person changing it is more senior. However, time constraints can mean that this linear review is not possible.

Another option is to send out the document saved in different names for individual reviews concurrently. Each must be set up with a direction to 'track changes'. The issue with this is you can end up with a whole lot of changes that are hard for you to incorporate whilst maintaining the flow of the document. If you choose to send the document out individually, check out the track changes>compare documents in Microsoft Word. It allows you to add track changes between versions of the same document and incorporate them into one document.

One thing that is guaranteed to make this process difficult is the person who has a fixed view on what is required in the application/bid. This person tends to have a particular mind-set, they are not keen to change their view and they can quite often change a win theme to a loss theme. You know who they are in your business? Right?

Dealing with this person is difficult. You can brief them on the RFT documents, you can share the agreed win themes, and you can advise them of the choice in the way the tender is written. However, if they are in a position of authority or lead in a specialist area, you may have to accept their changes and go with it. If this is the case, get that information in writing and unpack it with the project team or at the internal assessment stage (see later).

As each of the participants of the review team edit the document, you should save their document to the *Drafts* Folder and update the primary draft document. Ask that they sign off on their changes and ask whether they wish to review the document again based on who it is going to next.

With all of the edits, learn the differences and expectations of your review team and incorporate them for your future writing. You will find within

your organisation people have individual requirements and desires for the business writing style based
on how they write and some can be quite focused on
how they want things written and presented.
Learning the requirements of your management team
is a good learning experience for writing the next
tender.

Remember at all times to read the document
through after each edit. Ensure the application/bid
still meets the specifications and has not lost the
voice or the win theme with the changes. Do not be
concerned to go back to the reviewer and state where
you feel they may have changed the tender with their
edits and be clear, in writing, as to what or why that is
the case. If they are adamant about keeping it that
way, then follow the process for the fixed-view
member as detailed above and keep their written
response in your *Correspondence folder*.

When the editing and proofing are complete,
update the draft application/bid and save it as the
latest version in your *Drafts* folder. Make a copy of
that into the *Ready for Submission* folder, or in the final
document/online portal.

CHECKLIST

- Have you established a review team for micro and macro reviews?
- Have you set up a linear or group edit process?
- Have you educated the review team on the expectations of the RFT and the editing process?
- Have you incorporated their feedback and saved their comments and feedback?
- Have you saved the final draft?
- Have you copied it to the *Ready for Submission* folder and updated the final application/bid?

SIGN OFF AND SUBMISSION

The submission process changes in accordance with whether it is you signing off on the tender as the authorised signatory or whether there is another person higher up on your hierarchical structure. In either case, this is the part of the process where it is time to make sure you have covered all the points of the RFT.

By this stage you will be dealing only with documents in your *Ready for Submission* Folder including the *Other Documentation*. You will have checked off all checklists, the editing will be complete, professional advice incorporated, internal and external stakeholders' advice added and the final application/bid will be in a finished offline application/bid document or in a word file ready for final input and submission in an online portal. As part of the tendering project time-lines, you will know if you have to send your final document to printers and have the means of submission highlighted and planned. The time the signatory endorses the application will have been factored into that process.

Sign Off

A few days before the planned signing, confirm with the signatory that they are aware of the appointment, have factored in time to read the RFT and the submission. See whether they would like you to attend and ask them to ensure there is a backup signatory in place should they not be able to sign at that time. The last thing you want near to the submission time is a signatory off sick with no idea of who can sign in their absence.

The documents are complex. The signatory must understand what they are signing as well as the process the application/bid has been through before reaching their desk. It may be prudent to prepare a project brief to assist them. Within this document, make it clear that any changes they require will have a time impact on the submission process. Also, be clear that ignorance to the contents of the document will not negate the terms of the potential contract. If they cannot be bothered to read the RFT or the application/bid or are time-poor, they are still bound by what is in it, if the business is awarded the tender, they sign the contract and take the work.

Attach to this the application/bid in the ready for submission format. Explain what happens to their approval and the process for submission. It may be that their email approving the document is enough for you to enter the details into the online portal and send it. It may be that they have to sign a page and this is then emailed or printed for submission. If you are just printing off a page for the added signature and are planning to add this to the final submission, make sure the page numbers align. It is easy to have the page ready, then a paragraph is added to removed and the page numbers are thrown out of sync. It happens and it is better to be aware of it at this stage so as to plan for it.

Submission

Allow yourself as much time as possible for the submission but, never so early as to miss the final addendum issued by the organisation.

The reality of the tender process is you will be constrained for time. Things will go wrong, people will get sick, aliens will land, etc. Maybe that final one is a stretch but you get the idea. Allowing yourself time reduces the need to rush. It removes stress. It removes the potential for mistakes.

Allow yourself enough time to enter information into the online submission portal or to get the files to the printers and couriered to the organisation in good time. Allow time for last minute issues or queries that come up as you are working on the final stages.

The tender process is unforgiving at this stage. If you are late, the online portal will close you out. If the physical delivery is late, your application/bid will not be accepted into the assessment process.

With time on your side, you have time to deal with the unexpected, the issues and the problems. You have a clear head to resolve them and to adjust to an alternative plan.

Once you submit your application/bid, you will receive a proof of submission and you will have the final document. Save these to your *Submitted* folder. These are the copies that cannot be amended and I suggest access to them is limited and any copies distributed are in a locked PDF version.

With that done, it is time to update your opportunity pipeline with the date of submission, the final application/bid amount, the date you expect to hear the result of the tender process and any other information that your business requires in the Opportunity Pipeline database/spreadsheet.

Once the application/bid administration is concluded, it is time to thank the team and provide them with the proof of submission and relevant access to the final documents. The last 'thank you' email, closes the tendering writing process and is an opportunity for everyone involved to know the job is complete.

It is also the time to set up the internal tender assessment process whilst you wait for the organisation to assess your submission. This keeps the team involved and lets them know there will be a process to improve the process for the next tender application/bid.

CHECKLIST

- Are you documents final and within your *Ready for Submission* folder?

Sign Off

- Have you checked with your signatory for the availability to sign?
- Have you identified a signatory in their absence?
- Have you prepared a brief for the signatory?
- Have you prepared the application/bid page or highlighting where they sign?

- Have they signed off on the application/bid?

Submission

- Have you allowed yourself time to submit?
- Have you submitted?
- Have you updated the *Submitted* folder?
- Have you updated your Opportunity Pipeline Database?
- Have you thanked the team and circulated the required proof of submission and application/bid document?
- Have you set up the internal review process?

TENDER ASSESSMENT

Once the application/bid is submitted, it moves to the assessment process. The tender assessment process has two parts: the external assessment of the tender by the organisation and the internal assessment and review of the tender done by you at a business level.

External Assessment

Within the RFT documentation, organisations will sometimes share their assessment framework. To ensure probity of their procurement process, they will have a procedure to assess all tender applications/bid equally. It may be based on a scoring allocation that can be weighted to the answers with more or less importance to their decision. It may be based on value for money, social outcomes or other important factors to the organisation.

It is essential that you, as a writer, make the assessors' life easier. You need to write to their particular way and in a manner expected of their level of professionalism and knowledge base. It is at this stage you can see why it is so important.

The assessors will be assessing multiple applications/bids similar in length and depth to yours. If they can assess your value, understand your win theme and build their understanding in a clear and linear way, you have more chance of a higher position in the ranking. It is not a guaranteed award. For that, you have to meet their assessment needs and score higher than the competition.

On the assessment panels, there is usually a high level of formality with a team of assessors brought together with wide and varied skill sets relating to the tender in question. Each normally has a clear scoring matrix and assess either their area of expertise or, in some cases, the document in its entirety. Secondary aspects are normally then appraised. For instance, an infrastructure project may select the best engineering designs and place them in order of preference, the secondary factor could be the value for money or track record. The results are then combined and the tender offering the best of both aspects is usually awarded. What you can surmise, is, the best design might lose out based on their costs and the cheapest tender may lose out based on their design. As a business, you may never know.

It is easy at this point, and many businesses do, to believe there is a bias in the process. I am sure this does happen as no amount of governance is 100% effective.

Rather than considering bias, consider why another business won the award. The businesses you see win again and again have earned it. You can earn an award too.

Your business brand, your track record and your networking within the business field does matter. One area that is also growing is your commitment to corporate responsibility. It is also an area the assessors are targeting more and more, especially in the government environment.

Governments are under pressure politically and financially to meet the social needs of their community. If they are spending money, they want it to go to keeping their community employed, keeping the funds in the locality and to supporting those furthest away from the employment market. They want to see their home environments pollutant free and making use of the natural resources locally. This will extend to your supply line and the business you procure from.

By contrast, some organisations will put cost above everything else and some businesses will also submit an application/bid at a loss to gain the work. It may be prudent for some businesses to take a loss on a tender for other value-added opportunities they can gain.

With this information, it is time to discuss your internal tender assessment process.

Internal Assessment

Whether you are awarded a tender or not, seek feedback from the organisation. Ask for their feedback on where your tender was strong or weak and where the others were stronger.

Set up a review team and make it clear at the start that it is a non-blame assessment process. As you will have seen from the external process, you could have written the best application/bid, put in the most realistic and cost-effective price and been undercut by a business taking a deliberate loss. Conversely, you may have areas where you can improve. Regardless of the reason, analysing and reflecting on the process will make your next application stronger. Blame and finger-pointing will not. It only leads to people working in fear and questioning themselves at every stage of the writing. It makes for a bad work environment and a bullying culture.

With your review team in place, unpack the feedback from the organisation and reflect on that feedback. Review the awarded organisation and see how they fared under the tender. Do not be scared to look at their annual reports, if they are available in the public domain, and see whether they are still making a profit, where they are strong and where they excel in their business. Honestly review your tendering processes and organisation. There will be elements of the tender you can use again and put in your arsenal of generic paragraphs. There will be areas where you can improve and where your process may need some adjustment for the future. Create an ongoing internal review flow process to continuously improve, invest in your staff and seek to understand each organisation's requirements.

You will continue to learn, develop and improve. The tender environment will demand it from you.

CHECKLIST

External Assessment

- Do you have an understanding of the external tender assessment process?
- Did you get feedback from the issuing organisation?
- If you were not awarded the tender, are you aware of the business awarded the tender?

Internal Assessment

- Have you set up an internal review team with a no-blame culture?
- Have you reflected on areas for improvement?
- Have you updated your generic information based on the review?
- Have you got a quality and improvement process to ensure success in future tender applications?

FINAL WORDS

I hope the RFT process is less daunting to you now. A methodical approach to the application/bid, with the support of your project team, will put you in a good position to win the tender. It is not guaranteed and with each submission you will improve your process, your writing, and your storytelling to develop win themes and gain the tender award.

This book is based on the processes I have used throughout my twenty plus years of writing and submitting projects and I have no doubt you will improve upon it.

As I said at the start of this book, tenders provide you with a fixed fee, for a fixed service/product, for a fixed term. They can provide you with business stability for a term that can offer your business an opportunity to enjoy economic sustainability, growth, and expansion as a socially responsible business respected in your local community.

It is at this point, I remind you that the writing of the tender is only the start of the opportunity pipeline. It is time to reflect on your journey. Review your tender process and adapt it for the next tender. Review the project team and the management process and build upon it. Ensure the procurement plan is in place and that everyone is aware of the process and to act, only if successful. You do not want any contract starting before the cash is in place. The final administration processes are updating your opportunity pipeline and passing the work onto the teams involved in managing the tender. Make them aware of the contractual obligations under the tender and garner their acknowledgment. This is the last information to be placed in your folder *Submitted*.

I wish you well in your tender writing journey and if you have any questions you can contact me through my website www.grantandtenderwriting.com.

Happy writing!

Caroline

CHECKLIST

- Have you set aside time to reflect on the tender writing journey?
- Have you updated the opportunity pipeline?
- Have you passed on the information and caveats to those involved in the post-award activity?
- Have you updated your folders?

ABOUT THE AUTHOR

I live in Brisbane, Australia with my husband and I am still active in the tenders and grants community.

I am never happier than when I am developing a proposal that offers people possibilities. One that empowers people or communities to move from their current reality to one where their lives are enriched.

In doing so, I have worked in areas that have truly stretched my own reality and in worldwide locations. Outputs in university research and development, education, social justice, health projects to social firm development and business innovation and heaps in between.

Over my twenty plus years developing and delivering projects, I have brought in millions of dollars in funding, assessed grants and tenders on panels, mentored people and have developed a web community called Grant and Tender Writing.

Tender Writing – A Simple, Clear and Concise Guide is a way to give back to the community and to share possibilities, inspiration and knowledge with all of you.

I love writing, assessing, mentoring, coaching and strategic planning. I am happiest when I work with projects close to my personal values.

I love to hear from my readers. If you want to know more check out my website www.grantandtenderwriting.com and check out the forum for ongoing support.

For more information
www.grantandtenderwriting.com
contact@grantandtenderwriting.com

CHECKLIST

- Have you reviewed the book?

Seriously, your review is important to others who may be considering the book and also to me as an author to know whether the book has been helpful to you.

Thank you!

Printed in Great Britain
by Amazon